CRUX *of* MARRIAGE

Mary Agbotoh

WESTBOW
P R E S S®
A DIVISION OF THOMAS NELSON
& ZONDERVAN

WestBow Press books may be ordered through booksellers or by contacting:

WestBow Press
A Division of Thomas Nelson & Zondervan
1663 Liberty Drive
Bloomington, IN 47403
www.westbowpress.com
844-714-3454

ISBN: 978-1-6642-6246-1 (sc)
ISBN: 978-1-6642-6247-8 (e)

Library of Congress Control Number: 2022905982

Print information available on the last page.

WestBow Press rev. date: 05/02/2022

Chapter One

 ⟨∽⟩

GROWTH

Human beings use senses in everyday activities that lead to pleasurable and useful outcomes. Every human has characteristics that are unique that help him or her to stand out. And all humans have parents or guardians in their homes, where they exhibit their characteristics. The choice of the home is not the children's. Children grow to find themselves among people who love and nurture them. They learn the principles that keep them together, and they inculcate their values and processes.

First, they receive the basic knowledge; they learn how their parents interact to keep the home running smoothly. They observe who does what, why, and when; how it is done; and for what purpose. They learn the family history.

When children go to school, they are introduced to the community history and that of other places. They learn how things are done in the community. It might be different from how things are done at home, and they have to understand the differences. As they interact at home and school, their character is gradually formed. They make daily decisions as they encounter situations. This is how it is throughout life.

We all discover things that we feel strongly about. We encounter people who make an effort to influence us, and some tell us what to do. We create personal traits and develop opinions about issues. Listening helps us to better understand issues and to make good and balanced decisions. Whatever decision we reach should lead to better judgment and actions in the future. As we make better decisions, we're able to form relationships. People are attracted to us, and we benefit from other people's decisions as well.

Our thoughtfulness causes people to gravitate toward us. We meet various people, and we unleash our power of choice—choice of friends, of places to go, and of things to do alone or with family and friends. We tend to choose what will complement us and make us feel good.

Good behavior has its merits. People gravitate toward it. Ignorance and laziness make people behave badly. We learn there are consequences to all decisions. If society is peopled with humans that desire being good, it breeds harmony and good neighborliness from one generation to another. Our homes are where we first learn how to interact and be good, how to love, how to commit to an idea, how to be tolerant of others' viewpoints, and what kindness is. In school, we learn more. We thereafter take all this learning into the world and create an atmosphere of conviviality, and we become exemplary.

At home, the parents usually lead by example. They earn their income by contributing to tasks in a designated area and use that income for daily needs. A home can have two income-earning adults or one income-earning adult. It is a choice, and the decision is reached by the people in charge of the home. Financial knowledge is important.

Parents also keep the home clean and prepare meals and make that available to all in the household. They teach hygiene to the children. Everyone cares in the family.

In the community, the same system is introduced. It cares for its members' resources, and these are allocated according to need and availability.

Spirituality is also taught at home. A healthy mind is a gift to its generation.

Whatever transpires at home transcends into the community. Community leaders generate resources with which they run the community. They have the requisite skills—people skills, empathy, and the ability to have big dreams—to perform the needed tasks.

Remember that the boy child and the girl child, though they have different physiology at birth, are not treated differently. The parents take care of them equally; they are fed, clothed, and nurtured. As they grow and go to school, they are taught the same subjects. Only their areas of core competencies separate them.

Continually using beneficial, thoughtful action in activities helps one stand out. This is not necessarily about being good or bad; it is about making the utmost effort in living experiences to proffer solutions to debilitating issues and eroding unfavorable instances in all situations.

Leadership is about proffering solutions to complex issues. Leaders are visionaries; they can see a pathway that will lead to less debilitating situations. Leaders work hard at enforcing the road map for success. They simplify daunting challenges with the use of skills acquired, which can be improved in every generation. Being thoughtful and caring could be necessary for great achievement, coupled with the ability to allocate resources and choose the right people with core competence in areas of need. Most of them work long and hard at their tasks throughout their lives; others learn to delegate or allow others to supervise.

Everyone works in their areas of competence to contribute to the big pie, but that is after the visionaries have laid the foundations with painstaking effort. All great accomplishments were first an idea in someone's mind; then that person worked on the idea and acquired the necessary skills and knowledge that helped in its execution. So many processes are formulated until the workable ones are found, leading to successful completion.

Completed projects abound in our world. They're the work of men and women who were committed to a cause that they believed would make life pleasurable; it has been so for many centuries. They were first called pioneers. They understood the fundamentals and purposefully went against the grain. Some of them died before achieving their quests but were able to choose successors.

Chapter Two

⁂

BRIDGE

One of the relationships humans crave is of an intimate nature. Dating is one way this can be achieved. The sole purpose of this period in life is to discover themselves and each other—their likes and dislikes and their values and life purposes. This is not so that either of them will re-create the other; instead, this is a building block for getting to the core of their beings. During this time, some erroneously trivialize the process by pretending to be what they are not, leading to dire consequences. If this period in a relationship is properly handled, however, they will know ahead of time what to expect.

There can be surprises in life, but the damages will be absorbable because love covers a multitude of a misdemeanors. Love is not the only requisite in a relationship; the other needs will evolve as time goes on and as changes take place.

It is important to note that a percentage of people always refuse to change, or they change at a very slow pace. This then calls for decisiveness with regard to which move to take at every stage of the relationship. The dating stage in a relationship is not a period for cross-examination. It is a period to learn, to enjoy, and to reach a conclusion. Couples need depth to understand each other, as some of their values might not be apparent initially.

As you get to know each other, you will be introduced to the other person's aspirations, and yours will be clearer. You also will learn whether the relationship can be developed—that is, can it evolve? Is the tempo sustainable? Do you agree about certain things that are important to both of you? It's also an opportunity to understand each other's worldview. As events unfold, you will learn what each of you is against in world affairs and what you love. The more you know of each other, the better for your relationship. It is a time to be open with your views. Of utmost importance is an understanding and agreement for there to be a future for the relationship.

There will be areas of agreement and disagreement. The areas of divergent views have to be studied and understood because these could become conflicting issues. Conflict does occur, mostly because of misconceptions. To clarify issues, the broader outlook should be addressed. There is nothing wrong with having an opposing view. What is wrong is not being accommodating to others' differing views. Find out if the views can be settled and explained and a peaceful resolution decided.

Conflict most often occurs because one person wants his or her views to be the dominant, acceptable point of view all the time. Sometimes, however, it takes a while before people can achieve agreement and cohesion. The peaceful resolution of issues that we so desire is achieved by a process that takes time and effort. This process requires us to learn to be tolerant. It could also cause us to be kind and forgiving, to eschew pettiness, and to not keep an account of wrongdoings.

Your attraction to someone, for whatever reason, should be understood for its purpose, and you must recognize that there is more to the human makeup. You should not judge humans by their appearance; you need to learn more through association to find out their values in relation to their experiences. This research could lead you to discover that some of their attributes complement yours. They could have some character traits that you admire. If you dislike some of their traits or attributes, it might stir something in you.

It's important to make up your mind and be accepting of the current realities. Reach a decision on the way forward. Dating cannot be forever. Accept that all humans are working toward perfection; we are all works in progress. Once you have found someone whose building blocks of life are acceptable to you, you must commit to a lifelong relationship.

Commitment is a good attribute to have in a relationship. It is holding on to the core values discovered at the dating stage of the relationship. These could be improved upon in the unfolding years— this produces a harmonious relationship. It then helps in achieving the Holy Writ postulation that one will chase a thousand and two ten thousand.

Benefits accrue when the values in marriage are harnessed. Both parties have to do the harnessing. They have to guard the relationship from outside influences that might want to disrupt their plans and aspirations. They also should work, continually and thoughtfully, to improve the framework of the relationship.

One of the benefits to enjoying marriage is companionship. In the beginning, the Creator made them male and female and said, "For this reason a man will leave his father and mother and be united to his wife. And they will become one flesh" (Genesis 2:24 NIV). They are no longer two but one. Therefore, what God has joined together, let no man separate.

Now the two share every day, thought, and outlook. They are in close proximity to share ideas and give candid opinions about issues.

They are able to address issues according to their present continuous living activity. This involves the ability to switch off and not compare what happens in their household with those of distant places. They see their home situation as unique in daily activities, all the while infusing quality principles that enable families to thrive and enjoy all that is available to them.

Commitment breeds companionship. When the partners in a marriage relationship have committed their union by undergoing all the paperwork and vows before clergy, families, and friends, it produces contentment and a sense of acceptance and understanding.

As the marriage progresses and evolves, however, there will be disagreements and misunderstandings, as well as enjoyable times. New ideas will be infused into the relationship; this is essential because two different people are learning to live as one entity. They should seek help from books and experts on marriage issues to help in overcoming challenges and to be better able to understand each other. Also, couples should be aware of what triggers conflict and work to reduce it by celebrating their victories along with the way—the ones that reiterate the values that brought them together.

Resources abound for help with problems in marriage, from the inception of the union throughout the marriage. The benefit of doing this is monumental. Its impact could be enjoyed by the unborn generation, particularly when such benefits are documented and taught to couples. At this point in the development of the world, no one should just endure marriage; it should be a thrilling experience. Fun and creativity is a common fixture for couples; some also have inculcated understanding into it.

The bottom line is that a union requires effort to succeed. This is easier to accomplish with the right mindset, which is also a plus for success. Couples learn to understand each other with time and can actually predict some of each other's actions. Appreciation of each other sets in. There is much laughter, joy, great communication of ideas, and peaceful coexistence with thoughtfulness, thereby causing couples to want to stick together and continually improve upon the positive activity in their day-to-day experiences.

What happens in their home translates into the community and, thereafter, into society. As a loving couple, they will be more concerned with finding a loving way to resolve conflict. In the same vein, a person with a natural knack for saving money will institute a way to stretch funds—in a way that will not undermine the couple's pleasure and lifestyle.

Your involvement with people becomes beneficial. People frown upon interference, such that they shift the core principle of a union negatively. There is a need to guard against interference at all times. Not everyone will accept the idiosyncrasies of your union, and they might want to teach you how to tackle some aspect of your home activity. Unless you have specifically asked for such help, their advice is not appropriate.

At other times, you could be tempted to discuss your home issue with a friend or an extended family member. This is also not a good idea, as others do not have the whole picture, which will translate to giving a biased solution, and that could lead to the demise of the marriage. The home is where the future will be birthed. If you want the future creation to be an improvement, instill the positivity that might be missing. This can be achieved by the creation of an amiable ambiance in the home, where there is a peaceful and joyful coexistence in a stable environment. If there was poverty in an earlier generation, the couples should work together on their finances to make the union fruitful so the home will enjoy abundance in an atmosphere of thrift, thereby building a thriving day-by-day living experience.

The sole purpose of marriage by the Almighty is to bring about order in the community and the society at large. It is an institution that can be easily replicated. The problem it faces is due essentially to human inability to adhere to its tenets. One of the tenets of marriage is a unity of purpose. This leads to peacefulness and other good causes. Refusal to adhere to its principles, however, leads to communication breakdown, unhappiness, lack of synergy, abuse, an unhealthy outlook, hardship, and a lot of negative vibes. These could also lead to esteem issues that could be avoided.

I am saying all these beautiful things about the marriage institution because I have experienced it and could not manage it. My attempt collapsed. I believe that I gave my all to it and was willing to learn more to become a better partner, but my partner was not willing to go on. He was not open to suggestions for improving our relationship. He could not explain the issue he was having; he just wanted out of the relationship. As the days went by, our union ceased to exist. He did only what he wanted and did not communicate in an understandable way so there could be resolutions of differences.

The Holy Writ is filled with the tenets of marriage and the benefit that will accrue. Though my relationship floundered, the unions of other people are successful. In my own situation, I always wondered if love was not enough. Then I wondered if my expectations of the union were too high. I patiently dealt with each issue as it arose, but there seemed to be no solution in sight because of my partner's stance.

Chapter Three

—— ❧ ——

BEGINNING

I woke up this morning and went to get the mail. There was an envelope from my husband. He had earlier called to inform me that I should expect a particular piece of mail. He had been away from home for the last three weeks. I opened the envelope, and the contents infuriated me. He had instituted divorce proceedings.

The marriage had so many "downs." We were always arguing, and he had called third parties to intervene—people who always acquiesced to his ways. Most of the time, they sided with him. We never had amicable discussions. The disagreement was never about finances. It was usually about his unavailability. I ran the affairs of the home by myself. We never discussed issues; I usually had to find solutions by myself.

By the time he arrived home, one event would have been overtaken by another, and a new one would be brewing. He was forever involved in projects. I was happy for him, and the family was rich because of his enterprising spirit, but I demanded his presence. I wanted more, but he never budged. He was unable to give more of himself—and now, this. I was not going to contest the divorce. I was desirous of a more involved relationship, which I believed he was able to give, but he did not agree.

A long time ago, a mutual friend had introduced us, and we were attracted to each other. He was friendly and attentive. He also was sociable; he did the right things and said the right things. I believed he was true and held promise. He was generous with his financial gifting, but I also noticed that he was mostly preoccupied with things he never discussed when we were together.

He told me that I was different from other women he'd met. I was straightforward and easy to have a conversation with, coupled with other qualities he liked in a woman. Life was good, and before long, he proposed. I was overjoyed. This was what I wanted. We set a date, and we were married.

Initially, he was loving and caring, and life was blissful. Then, I began to notice that he usually wasn't present in thoughts. I let it slide, but the more I kept quiet, the more disturbed I became. So I brought it up. "Let's talk about it," I said.

He explained it as the nature of his business.

What could I do? I got busy with other aspects of our lives. In hindsight, that was a mistake. We started having our children, and then we spent our days with family and friends and working hard at our jobs. He spent most days away from home, and I took the children with me to church. The words of the Lord soothed my being.

How would I explain my recent situation? I mentioned it eventually to one of the elders. I was thereafter led in a series of prayers—encouragement about the love of God, for he promised that he would not leave us or forsake us. God will be with us at the very end of time.

What I wanted in marriage, aside from love and security, was companionship. I never had it. It was an elusive element that I missed. I buried myself in work and took care of the home. I moved from one activity to another, looking for an escape. I did not have an answer for what was troubling me, so I wished the trouble away. When my mind tried to stray, I thought about what to do. I stilled my mind and concentrated on what I was doing. I became very efficient at what I was about, but the issue with my husband lingered. I quelled it sometimes with food. I became adept at looking for things to occupy my time.

I let myself go; I became someone else. Most of the time, I just went through the motions of life. Although I spoke with my husband about us and sought help from established sources, I never went by myself when he refused to accompany me.

And now, there was this letter from him.

On his part, he told me he'd had a discussion with his friends and acquaintances who saw things from his own angle. They told him he should move on with his life.

I concluded that he rejected the established input for the challenges we were facing because the benefits of his hidden activities outweighed the benefit from our union. This affected my self-esteem. I recalled feeling ashamed of myself in other relationships. I believed I had failed to make a success of what I wanted the most. I started a comparison system of my relationships. I condemned myself and belittled whatever positive contribution I had made in the past. Though I gave all my attention, focus, and care, it was not enough. I did not have the blissful ending I had envisioned.

Then one day, I realized that I alone did not bring about the demise of the relationship. He also contributed. He did not accept what I wanted; he refused to acknowledge my outlook on life. Therefore, he could not continue living with me. I believe I was not asking for too much, but now, I think that was probably part of the problem.

Also, he wouldn't tell me what preoccupied him, and he never gave me a choice in his decision. He made up my mind for me; he refused to be present or to be involved in a manner that I wanted. I hoped for a change; it never came. I occupied my time with the task, wishing that my need for his presence would erode away.

But it never went away. It led to frustration, which I manifested by bickering. There was no choice; he ignored me and continued with his choice of action. It is so unbelievable that someone who was so accepting at the beginning of our relationship could turn out to be so distant and uninvolved. *How can this be happening?* I wondered.

Then he started traveling and was gone for days, then weeks, on business; then for the extended family programs, projects, and functions. His desire to be away was unending. I realized that love didn't live here anymore, and I was *alone*. The bliss I'd dreamed of at the beginning had evaporated. *Am I imagining things?* I wondered. *No, it is real. Though I am in a union, I am the only actor.*

The other person had become a bystander. Who would save me? What would I have to do? It was usual for me to have dumbfounded days—days when we did not communicate. We were not busy with anything, but we had nothing to say to each other. After returning from a trip, he never talked or shared anecdotes about his travels—not about his business or his encounters. Then it dawned on me that I had been the one, most of the time, initiating conversations and sustaining them. I had been the only one sharing experiences. Whatever information about him I had garnered had been true intuition or gut feelings. This discovery annoyed me.

Then I asked myself what had attracted me to him. Did I become involved with him because of youthful exuberance? Had I lacked the understanding to choose someone to spend my life with? Or had events happened to kill the love and understanding we once shared? I couldn't explain how we got to this point, where we were nonchalant about building a fruitful and engaging relationship.

I made an effort to reignite our togetherness; I believed in us. The attribute must be embedded in us somewhere in our minds, I reasoned.

I still loved him and believed he was a good man, although he could be better. He, however, gave up. He made no effort to be involved. He was distant and would not communicate. He refused to share his life with me. My joy and my needs were meaningless to him. *I wish I knew what to do*, I thought.

My efforts bore no good results. He refused to go with me to seek help. Crossing this bridge alone, I discovered that it would not be enough to sustain a workable relationship. I needed him to cross it with me; he refused. I always had believed that my marriage would last a lifetime, but I realized that wishing for that wasn't enough; you have to work at making it a reality. You have to devise a strategy to keep a relationship alive and lovely.

A relationship is the coming together of two people with defined characteristics, most times with divergent views or life experiences. Therefore, allowances must be made for a newness together. There should be no room for a rift. Instead, there should be a building up of camaraderie and understanding of each other's character traits, thereby recognizing areas of differences and similarities for the enjoyment of a great and joyous lifestyle. If this is achieved, one has a companion for life.

That would mean I would always have someone who would be helpful. I have realized that everyone needs help at some point in life. If you have someone helpful and committed as your better half, it is a blessing. You can celebrate your milestones together and celebrate memories. These serve to strengthen bonds and give you something to reminisce about. This, then, creates a situation whereby you could do good for the love of your life.

You thoughtfully plan and create a life worth living with someone you care for. You also make amends in the process of living by apologizing and making it right by your partner always. This creates a great atmosphere at home, where humor and laughter are already residents. So as the years go by, you look for opportunities to do good things for each other. Your spouse and the marriage institution will thrive under this atmosphere.

The changes that occur as the years go by will be welcome and celebrated. The areas of conflict should also be dealt with, using the right perspective. No untoward situation should be allowed to fester and degenerate to a full-scale acrimonious situation. Constant communication is needed.

There should be a clear train of thought at all times in order to prevent adverse conditioning of the relationship or dissolution of what was started on a good note. All relationships need the investment of time, money, and effort. Concerted moves should be instituted to prevent bitterness and the concealment of true intent. These will stall the forward movement of all that is good in the relationship. If this situation inadvertently happens, adverse results might occur. Some relationships never recover and will end on a negative note.

Those who suffer most when such a relationship ends tend to view everyone through the prism of the partner in the failed union. Sometimes, they erroneously conclude that it is their fault and that they are no good for anyone. They continue to hurt themselves. This outlook might create a devastating action in their future relationships. Such people need counseling to help them to understand what happened.

It's not enough to have a public party to celebrate a marriage. Both partners in the marriage need to make an effort to be good to each other and society. They must always celebrate their strengths and work at improving their weaknesses. They can creatively inculcate this into their lifestyles. This will cause the relationship to thrive, and areas of conflict will be minimized and ameliorated in love. It leads to the understanding of views and outlooks.

When conflicts arise in the future, both partners will remember how former conflicts were resolved and seek to return to the procedure used to solve former conflicts. Although there will be differing circumstances, they still can use the basics of dialogue, communication of the perceived issue, and patience in finding a longtime solution. The parameters for resolving the issue in the home lead to peaceful coexistence in the home and greater understanding among spouses.

The thinking pattern of each partner is easily discernible, and it becomes easy for partners to anticipate outcomes. This, then, becomes an ingenious way of fortifying a relationship. This process of achieving mutually beneficial solutions to conflicting issues causes both parties to reiterate their beliefs and values and makes it easier to clarify gray areas as it pertains to expectations. Each spouse might be tempted to discuss issues in the marriage with friends and family members; this is not advisable. It is much better to use the services of accredited counselors. Friends of the marriage partners should not be bogged down with the conflict between the spouses, as they are usually not trained to solve marital problems, and they might take the side of the one with whom they are most friendly.

Once you are married, boundaries must be maintained. Marriage was created to be a harmonious relationship. At the inception of the institution, a man was made to sleep, and one of his ribs was removed and used to create the woman of his dream. Because of the same substance their makeup, they are expected to understand each other, which they do—that's why they chose each other in the first place. They should not allow men to put asunder what God has joined together. They are encouraged to have a singleness of purpose and to procreate through the enjoyment of the sort of intimacy of which God approves. A new family is birthed.

Chapter Four

⸺ ❧ ⸺

SINGLE AGAIN

I felt pain at the demise of my marriage. The dream of a fun-filled homelife was not successfully actualized. I experienced a period of excitement while it lasted, although short-lived, and I will count that as my blessing.

I will look to the future with optimism. My former partner, through the hardness of his heart, refused to use the available resources to find a solution to the issues that arose in our relationship. This created a dismal homelife that made togetherness and joyful coexistence unachievable.

On my part, I kept questioning myself on what we could have done differently. I remembered the times I cried and pleaded with God to intervene and make things right.

Now, we have both moved on, and I have a new resolution and outlook. I will communicate my true feelings and thoughts in a cordial manner. I will leave room for the discussion that will ensue and the conclusion that will be reached. I will always seek clarity for what I do not understand and explore all avenues for its exposition. Then, my actions will be based on my learning.

I wish the same outlook for those who have similar situations to my relationship. I also want us to deal with present issues that will have future benefits, rather than running ahead into future possibilities. I believe that when we deal with present issues, future issues become clearer.

I will seek to understand and be understood. I will not procrastinate. In the past, I knew there was a problem with my marriage, but I kept postponing seeking help from dedicated counselors until it was too late. I am now committed to dealing with issues as they arise.

I will add creativity to my actions. I will have fun and try to see the funny side of life. I will take time to retreat, to ponder, and to create scenarios, which is a way for me to learn how things might be. I believe this will help me to achieve desired outcomes. This will ensure that I please myself within the outcomes of what is permissible. I will seek to take advantage of the changes that happen by exploring more opportunities in my areas of interest and capabilities.

In hindsight, maybe I should have gone on those trips with my husband. Joining him on a trip occasionally might have produced a different outcome. Still, I have no regrets whatsoever. It has been a learning process of why he made the decision to leave. I lost the knowledge I would have gained about his business if I had gone with him. Instead, I moped around the home, wishing he would spend quality time with us.

With this resolve, I am very enthusiastic about the future. I have prepared a balanced and knowledgeable outlook on how to forge a relationship. With this perspective, I conclude I will have a very interesting lifestyle. I will keep seeking learning opportunities in my areas of interest. This will help to expand my experiences. I will not only learn but will organize and will incorporate my new knowledge, effectively and efficiently, into my activities and areas of interest.

I promised myself that I will not be overwhelmed by circumstances but will be proactive and operate from an optimum level. I will welcome new experiences and learn the requisite lesson taught; then I will move quickly with that lesson to my next endeavor. I will continue to hold myself accountable for my actions to ensure I am a better human, privately and in my community.

Likewise, I will not overlook people's behaviors but will accept that whatever behaviors they exhibit are the best they can muster at the moment. By seeking training opportunities and researching areas of interest, I will have a better understanding of situations and issues.

Detachment is a concept I am finding useful. By this, I mean not imposing my ideas on others but allow the other person in the relationship to get to the same page with me. Meanwhile, I will keep improving myself within available resources, without diminishing my present or future happiness. This process aids self-discovery with purpose, which leads to the fundamental question of why I want what I am yearning for. What would be its benefit to me in present terms and in the future? Who am I becoming by the desires that plague my mind?

The realization dawned on me that my failed experience at marriage was an opportunity to discover myself again. Life has bestowed on me the opportunity to achieve a newness hitherto unknown to me—to live a fruitful and productive life; a life that contributes and harnesses opportunities to the fullest.

It is my belief that the earth is peopled with unique and diverse beings with the immeasurable capacity to contribute and take advantage of wide-ranging chances to create favorable circumstances, while, at the same time, seeking ways to explore and improve themselves and the community. The differences in communities complement and complete all.

Some people, however, do not know how to tap in to the good in society. They could start by emulating credible people on the way to discovering their hidden and untapped uniqueness, realizing that its benefit would be monumental. It is akin to being a single person—a period, if well used, that will help one unearth one's own uniqueness.

As you explore every day alone, you realize the unique *you*. You form your alone characteristics that may have been unrealized. Being single likely will not be a forever state; it will surely come to an end. This is because humans were created for connection. This realization helps us to situate our uniqueness for exponential increase and fulfillment in our daily activities and future plans.

It is incomprehensible to me that some people seek to thwart this human connectivity by their mediocre thoughts and actions. Singleness ends because of the intricate needs of humans, although it's advantageous in being the gestation time for the development of unique ideas and characteristics. It also serves to prepare us for the eventual unification with another being, with the sole purpose of continued goodness to ourselves and the larger society.

The earth is peopled with beings who have unique and diverse capabilities, and there is a dimension of understanding that is still being explored. There is still room for exploration in one's area of interest; this is so one becomes a contributor. In doing so, a level of competence is exhibited in a certain stratum of society.

To be accomplished in a chosen field, an understanding of societal values is imperative—its norms and the vehicle for achievements of ideals—not in a biased way but in a balanced manner. To do this effectively, we need to be less judgmental and accept that things are evolving. Change should be welcomed as a vehicle that reenacts the activities of all humans. The time when we are single could be likened to a period of recuperation, when we are alone with thoughts that filter through our minds. It's also like when we retreat from everyday life to deeply think of issues that constantly bombard the mind, helping us to reach favorable conclusions in an unobstructive way. The decision that is reached still has to be tested against the current situations.

There is joy in fellowship, and humans do yearn for that fellowship because it leads to abundance; that is one of the benefits of cooperation. It also creates improvement in human endeavors. Connection is an important component in a relationship so that it can thrive.

Being single while on an explorative journey of discovering strength and its purpose prepares us to make decisions on how to resolve weaknesses that we identify.

Chapter Five

———— ❧ ————

REMARRIAGE

There is a need for self-analysis when the first attempt at married life fails. It should be a no-holding-back process. Tell the whole truth. This will lead to an action-and-consequence revelation. Accept whatever you discover without giving excuses. This will help you to take the action step to move on and to be prepared for a new relationship.

Purge all thoughts that hinder thoughts. Also purge the actions that lead to past failures, and embrace the newness that becomes available. Forgive yourself and your partner so that unforgiveness will not harm new relationships.

Avail yourself of the possibilities in the world. Rid yourself of the desire to relive the past; lay the past to rest. Let your mind know that you have undertaken a new journey that is a fresh start to life and that you can accomplish a great feat. The newness for which you wish should be accompanied with bliss.

A self-audit then becomes necessary. It is imperative that the mind be free of thoughts of past failings. This is possible by the creation of new system and by being involved in challenging activities that broaden the mind, such as new interests. Approach these activities with an open mind for learning. Seek the opportunity to contribute, with a mindset that is prepared for changing or expanding expectations that can accommodate new learnings.

Also be prepared for certain action and events that could lead to improvement, such as certain acts that could go from good to excellent. Such discovery is exhilarating. This sort of discovery is what we want to take into our relationships. Concerted effort should therefore make our affairs attractive, whereby we ask ourselves pertinent questions and realign our purposes and core beliefs to meet the standardized mode of behavior in our community or the one to which we wish to belong.

For example, if we have overdrawn our credit, and it has become impossible to save and invest because of credit payments, we have to fix those discrepancies before we seek a meaningful connection. We must always seek to put our best foot forward, particularly at the inception of a relationship. This depicts maturity in dealing with life experiences.

Taking these steps shows we are ready and able to connect positively. Life then becomes monumentally enjoyable. This is the point where there is excitement for the unusual events that life brings forth.

There are systems and measures of performance of life tasks that bring about success. This also applies to relationships. It should not be a dogma; we can disagree at any point. There are areas of disagreement and agreement in all established systems, thereby leading to a positive conclusion. The outcome of these processes is mutual respect for all parties involved. The recognition and appreciation of beneficial attributes, in an atmosphere that is devoid of rancor and rivalry, only seeks the good of the other in every circumstance. Don't compare yourself with others.

Disagreements are seen as such, which could become strengths. Always be careful not to harp on the differences that are brought to the relationship. As the relationship evolves, the point of disagreement will keep thinning if you make deliberate effort to work on improving, and the issue is understood better. Disagreement will become nonexistent. Both partners will resolve to work for the best outcome. All negativity will be chiseled away by positivity. Areas of conflict will be seen from a productive standpoint. Partners will preempt themselves and make an effort for joyful coexistence in a fun-filled atmosphere.

Fun and creativity should be built-in areas of interest. That leads to a lot of laughter and creativity, which could lead to travels to places that evoke pleasant memories, discovering memorabilia and the sharing of anecdotes. This creates conversation, which further bonds you for life. The purpose of this is to expand the sphere of life, an attempt to move from the mundane to the thrilling; to loosen up and get away from the everyday regimen of work life and the hardcore routine that involves critical thinking.

From what I can remember of the fun times while I was married, they were periods spent in the midst of people. In hindsight, I see that as our relationship progressed, he avoided being alone with me. Was he scared that I would brainwash him? I never knew, as he became economical with his thoughts. It is unimaginable that our relationship became one where we had nothing to say to each other.

I find myself trying to recollect how our union started. With deep reflection, I came to the realization that there *were* clues at the very beginning. He was always going off to make a call. He was never wholly present. I did not know what that meant back then. I was so much in love that I lost my discerning ability. I could not interpret these events to mean that he would never be fully involved.

He had no apology. He accepted that he could never be so enmeshed in our relationship as to give all.

Can I have more? I wondered. *And should I ask for all I need? Like total involvement?*

I believe so now. I did not deserve to be with one who had decided, ahead of time, on the percentage of his involvement in our living arrangement.

I believe in an excellent lifestyle and to be the best in whatever I choose to do. I do not believe in half measures and a haphazard way of doing things. Fun times usually are when we allow others to provide service or entertainment at a fee. This is so we can enjoy some of life's bounty.

After a season of hard work, we need to let off steam. Some go for a massage to loosen the tightening in various parts of the body. Others attend shows or concerts or listen to soothing music. And those who can afford it may take a vacation—this is a great way to unwind, if done properly, because it enables vacationers to take time off from busy schedules and only do what they enjoy the most.

There are so many vacation spots in the world. With proper research, one could discover the best place for any individual, family, or group. Vacationers are well advised to immerse themselves and enjoy the environment and all it has to offer. It is a time where others are the actors and are set up to give an enjoyable time—to entertain and help vacationers forget all the difficulties in the workplace.

Work is a constant for us; therefore, we should have a good work ethic always. Productive work powers all the great institutions and establishments in the world, and the usefulness of such cannot be overemphasized. It brings about an increase in revenue and the development and production of infrastructures for the betterment of all humans. It also leads to the harnessing of profitable ventures. It has contributed to the development of standardized conditions in the world.

Rules and regulations guard the work environment that have helped workers take caution and not hurt themselves. Continuous work is prohibited; break time is built into the shift. This is a time to refresh and reflect on what has been accomplished in the day and to project toward the future impact of what is yet to be done. Each organization chooses what it believes is best for its workforce. Workers, in most cases, are encouraged not to take work home. This measure is to help in eliminating burnout, as overwork has been found to negatively impact the health of workers.

People are encouraged to work in their areas of interest and passion in the long run. Much as there is specialized training for the workforce, they are to train and retrain, as the need arises, at a pace they can well manage. They have to plan and organize to be able to partake in these processes.

Organization of time is also critical. There are a lot of resources on time management. Time is a finite resource; we must use it wisely. Planning, organization, and delegation are useful and should be studied and used at all times, in all facets of our lives, for efficiency and effectiveness.

We do not need to repeat the mistake of others. We can scale through this when we use the lessons of those who have passed through processes before us. This can aid in our learning what we need. There are so many resources to choose from. It rests on us to search for what we want.

It is very costly to repeat the mistakes of the past. We are only allowed to learn from history, not repeat it, and to improve ourselves.

Some people bury themselves in mundane work when they focus on difficulties inherent in life, and they do so to the exclusion of the benefits in various ventures. For such people, the focus on routine gives them a modicum of security, but it's to the exclusion of taking risks in new and exciting ventures. Work becomes an escape from reality for such people.

Whatever ails a human has a solution. Work should be of the sort that produces positive benefits, a result that is quantifiable. We should not spend hours going through the motions, which does not produce value in the long run.

My former partner and I had a different view of what work should be. I keep regular hours, as there is another type of work for me—house chores. When I could not get through to him, I hid my thoughts behind doing chores around the house. I would spend an entire morning in the kitchen or a day reorganizing the bedroom—time that could have been used to strategize, to think positively about our plans for the future, or to jest and laugh in the home, instead of being cut off from the happenings in the home.

For him, it was work throughout the day. Every other relationship took second place. He only stopped once in a while to do other things. His phone was never far from him, and he would stop whatever he was doing to answer his phone. He never complained when the phone rang; he anticipated calls. It was a way of life that worked for him.

We are living apart now. I appreciate this arrangement, for it will enable me to redefine myself and put my priorities in the right perspective. I am not my only focus; I have my children to think about—two teenage boys and a girl, seven years old. I got custody of them; he did not contest it.

Sometimes, I catch my daughter, staring. I hope they do not repeat my mistakes. I will be a role model for them. They have become clingy since learning about our family situation. I am lost as to what questions to ask them. For their sake, I promised myself that I would be courageous and strong through the transition, which will establish us as a single-parent family—a mother living with her children.

People were quick to tell me that they wished I would find a soul mate. I could not discern why this was their wish for me. I had no such desire myself. What I wanted above all else was to forge a stable family life for us.

I want to be able to reassure my children that we can have a loving family life, where our dreams will be realized. Initially, we began a process of enriching our values and adjusting our lives. The process was costly, but I was able to formulate a short-term and long-term workable system for us. I desire that my children will know that life does happen; that one has to make best use of what is happening and to learn the lesson therein and grow from it. I also want them to know that life lessons are always happening. That is how growth takes place.

They should ask, "What has happened? What role of mine brought this to pass? What is its effect on me and all that is mine? Am I comfortable with its effect? Am I willing to change the aftermath? Who can be helpful and for what purpose?"

The purpose of our family is to assuage whatever hurt is locked in the recesses of our minds and to continue to live our lives successfully. I've helped my children to realize that as long as they are living beings, there will always be issues to resolve. They should embrace the process of seeking resolution and not to shy away from it.

Now they have new schedules, but I will always be available to answer their questions and make their lives as easy as possible, but I'll be firm when I need to be. I'm bringing them up in ways that will be beneficial to themselves and to society at large. They will become individuals who deal with challenges head-on and apply themselves to what has to be done.

They were quite accepting of the arrangements I made and were happy to reside with me. With that settled, I concluded that our best life is ahead of us. As might be expected, the reaction of family and friends was mixed. Some encouraged me to remarry quickly so that I would have a man to do the manly things around the home. I did not accept their point of view; although they didn't know it, the end of my marriage was not sudden. I had to do a lot of things that he used to do before the end. I was more in tune with those people who encouraged me to rediscover myself before I started dating so that my actions would not be reactionary.

I believe this is my time to rejuvenate myself. I welcome this time with anticipation and trepidation and optimism. I believe it is a gift to be able to start over. Although I, in no way, wanted a divorce, I am committed to making a success of my life, now more than ever before. Some people believed I should have let him keep the children, that he deserved a disrupted life and at least an iota of hardship. But when I thought of all the disruption his actions had caused so far, I knew that the children would be better off with me.

I chose the path of peace because of my faith and my children. They needed close monitoring, attention, and nurturing. The arrival of children always changes so much in a couple's lifestyle and expands their sphere of activities. As children grow, they learn from their parents' examples, not necessarily from what they say but what they do. This helps them to create a tranquil and better environment later in life.

Parenting involves a lot of care and work. Not only has there been an overhaul of our lifestyle because of our circumstances, but my vocabulary and circle friends have been affected by the changes. All in all, we came out stronger, with an expansive and broader outlook. The children have exhibited an understanding that has belied their ages. They have taken responsibility for whatever they had to do without complaining. We all have transitioned seamlessly into the new experience life thrust at us.

I did not display an outward show of animosity toward my former spouse; we simply did not have anything to say to one another anymore. I only shared my life with the children. They would speak with him, and nothing changed between them or between him and us. There was no show of emotion, just the usual exchanges and being dutiful and respectful. The children seemed content and accepting of what the routine would be, particularly when he would be able to visit with them.

I learned whatever I needed to know from the official deliberation of our case. Being apart is the best option for us; whatever we had before could not be resuscitated. Now, we have an opportunity to reenact our lives and seek new meaning for our existence so we won't fixate on what is not working. This is only possible if we form new relationships, which will enable other experiences that will propel us into a future that we want.

I shy away from discussing him with the children. I only listen to what they have to say about him. They are still young and impressionable. I do not want to influence their opinion of him. It should be theirs to have.

For the most part, my friends and colleagues shared some life lessons with me—their unfortunate incidents and how they overcame them. I was grateful for the encouragement. These made me more aware of the people and the community in which I have been living and working. Some said they were available whenever I needed to talk—and talk I did. I bared my mind to some of them and wondered why I had not sought such release sooner. I cherished their wealth of wisdom. It is amazing that all these good people were around all the time I was pining for a connection. This is my time to connect with other humans and to enjoy pleasures untold.

Chapter Six

SECOND ACT

I was in the eatery near my workplace, lost in thought, when a man, carrying his tray of food, pulled out the chair across from me.

"Do you mind if I sit at your table?" he asked.

Because I took my time before answering, he was already seated when I said, "Not really ..." What else could I have said?

I kept on eating, deciding to ignore him.

He had other ideas. "I've noticed you in the past," he said amiably. "This seems like an opportune time to get to know you."

I kept on eating silently, totally ignoring his remark. I did look at him and decided he was middle-aged, like me. He was handsome and seemed to be a nice man. He continued to eat while I scrutinized him.

I could not remember having seen him before this, even though I usually had lunch at this same eatery, which was very close to my office. Even though he took the initiative to approach me, he seemed the quiet type. Though we were focused on our meals, we were keenly aware of each other.

"I am George."

"I'm Debora. My friends call me Debbie."

We exchanged pleasantries. He happened to work in the same block of offices where I worked and seemed to know my schedule.

"I've noticed you usually come here for lunch," he told me.

"Yes, I do. It's convenient."

George nodded. "I do most times as well. I enjoy the food."

"I enjoy the food as well."

"Could we spend a few minutes at the park nearby after our meal sometime?" he asked.

"Yes, we can do that sometime."

"Could we eat a packed lunch at the park instead of eating in the restaurant?"

I smiled at him. "That would be a good idea as well."

This was the first man I'd spend time with since my divorce. He behaved in an agreeable manner. I learned that, like me, he was divorced.

He informed me that his divorce was hurtful. His wife fought to get all his money, which he accepted because of their child. He said that the more she got, the more she wanted. She left him with an emotional scar and fear of trusting women. "But like I said, I've been continually drawn to you from the day I first noticed you at the eatery."

As much as I tried to veer the conversation away from ourselves to various topics, he always found ways to bring it back to us. I told myself I was not ready for a relationship at that point, but every workday, we were at the same spot, eating our lunch.

He told me about his favorite food, which he enjoyed in a variety of ways; it was made at the eatery. He also told me that he would love to travel if he had the means to do so without incurring debt.

I seized the opportunity to let him know that I had an upcoming vacation with my children. "It's our first since the divorce," I said, "and I'm really looking forward to it."

He seemed disturbed by this information. "I'll miss our time together," he said.

I did not comment on that, but his demeanor compelled me to tell him that the organization I worked for had other plans for me on my return. "I will be transferred to a larger section of the organization and will have more responsibility," I said. "Most often, that will erode the luxury of a lunch hour outside the office."

He was visibly saddened by the information but said, "On your return, we will find and plan our future meetings."

I agreed but could not envision how we would do that. Aside from work and time spent with my family, I also spent some of my time in church. It was a place where my spirit was fed weekly. Usually, there was a program of events; there was one recently for singles that caught my attention. I was curious enough to plan on attending.

On the appointed day, the venue, which was ordinary, had been transformed. The place was packed with astoundingly well-dressed men and women. I scanned the program of events, and a particular game caught my attention—it was for singles who came as couples. They were asked to come to the podium. Each couple was asked a series of questions, which was to determine what they knew about each other. It was a hilarious as they realized that they didn't know as much about each other as they had assumed. It was a revealing exercise to all participants. The host suggested that the couples had a lot to learn.

I also took time off to attend a seminar on personal finances. All I seemed to do was spend from my paycheck, and the remainder was left in my account. I went to the seminar to learn how to invest for the future. So far, my only investment was our house and a huge collection of jewelry.

While I was married, I was more concerned that we have great experiences, sparing no expenses, particularly with the children. I went to the seminar to seek ways of spending less while having a great life and having something significant saved for later life.

I was made to realize that I had to get the children involved. I learned a lot of tidbits for my children, which translated to the consequences of not having money. I taught them ways for stretching our money and using delayed gratification. They were happy for the changes in our financial life and were enthusiastic about budgeting. They were agreeable to the idea of keeping an account of our spending. I believed this would curb some of their demands for items.

The plan we drew was for 70 percent of our income for living expenses and 30 percent saved. We loved the idea of having money saved up for future use. We agreed that no one would complain when we wore some of our clothes a little longer or when we did not buy the latest toy. We also agreed that we would be practical and go to places where we could relax and rejuvenate at lower costs. We discovered we would be able to consistently do so, if we planned ahead.

Once I had the understanding, it was easy to discuss with the children the changes required for a better standard of living. I searched for healthy foods, which I introduced to them. I also encouraged little things that would be beneficial eventually—like brushing their teeth twice daily. We also took time to celebrate our success, after a well-thought-out plan of the cost implications.

In the long run, I realized that I needed to increase my income, which piqued my interest in an entrepreneurial seminar. I attended, and it was well worth it. I had mixed feelings about setting out on my own. I was afraid of the amount of work I would have to do. Then I thought about the effort required for mastery. My fear faded, however, when I decided to focus on what I love doing. I love reading, so I decided to sell books. The easiest platform was online. I made up my mind to learn how to operate an online store. I believed that with training and exposure, I would achieve the how-to.

So I started. I had to wade through a lot of written materials. I understood that hoisting would be the best experience for me because I was new. I had to overcome my initial fear and invest in a training program, in which I walked over the entire process from start to finish, thereby dissolving most of my fears. I realized there was still a risk; there were no guarantees. I had to continually improve my actions and thoughts to achieve eventual success.

The process, though cumbersome, was interesting. Picking the domain name created in me the love of ownership—but I was aware that profitability was a long way off. And I resolved that, for now, this would be a part-time business. I still had to go to my regular employment; it enabled me to meet my responsibilities.

I resumed my job with an appreciation of the establishment that employed me. The place afforded me a good income over the years, with the opportunity for a rejuvenating vacation. As I resumed work, it was with much gusto that I immersed myself in my daily schedule. This also involved having meetings where we deliberated and brainstormed on projections that would bring about growth and profitability.

As I had told George, my new schedule involved more responsibility that affected our being able to meet for lunch, so we met briefly after work.

"Good to see you," I said, smiling when I saw him.

"Missed you," George told me—and my smile broadened. "Lunch was not the same without you."

"I had a well-deserved break and rest," I said.

"You look rested and as beautiful as ever."

"Thank you."

"Tell me—which wonderful sight did you behold?"

I laughed out loud.

"You can't just laugh. Tell me."

"I went mountain climbing."

"Really? That sounds like work."

"I enjoyed it."

"What made it enjoyable?"

"The thrill!"

"Did you jump or leap to the mountaintop?"

"I leaped!"

"Interesting," he said. "I missed you."

"Really? What did you miss about me?"

"The way your eyes light up."

"Just that?" I asked.

"Your smile awakens a sensation in me," he said.

"Seriously?"

"Your presence makes me happy. You did not return my call."

"I was too busy to call," I insisted.

"Busy? Busy at what?"

"Sorry. I was busy with so many things."

"It was your vacation."

"It was a combination of relaxation time and learning new things."

"Do you want to talk about that time?" he asked.

"Yes, but not today. I enjoyed my time off."

"Glad for you."

"Good. So how are you?" I asked.

"I missed you, all the while spending time with my tech toys."

"Any new discovery?"

"Millions! I have tons of information."

"Then we are buddies after all."

"What do you mean?"

"I need some tech training," I admitted.

"No! No! I am not going to train your pretty head."

"Why not?"

"I have better things to teach you."

"What better things?"

"You want tech training?"

"Yes!"

"Not from me," he insisted.

"Why not?"

"Training you?"

"Who said training me?" I asked.

"Good. Nobody said it."

"Good." I stood up and started to leave.

He caught me. "Why are you in such a rush?"

"I'm running late for my next appointment."

"Time runs so fast when I am with you."

I smiled.

"You are beautiful!" George said.

I smiled more.

"You see that it is good and fantastic."

We said our goodbyes. The relationship was interesting. George was willing to talk and spend time with me, but he also wanted to connect with me. "Am afraid to commit?" I asked myself. "I must admit that I like his company and enjoy the attention he gives me. But I have to tread with caution this time around."

I had not been able to understand why a loving and giving friend would suddenly turn the other way, and nothing would make him rethink his decision of wanting a permanent disengagement.

The next time I saw George, I broached a question that was gnawing at my mind. I began by telling him, "I appreciate you."

"Well, yes, that is great to know."

"We appear to be good together."

"Yes, we are!" George agreed.

"We always have something to talk about."

"I agree."

"Our conversations are candid."

"Yes, they are, and I love your enthralling smile."

"What, then, causes the end of such beautiful liaisons?" I asked.

"The breakdown of communication causes it," he answered.

"What causes the breakdown of communication?"

"A lackluster outlook on the relationship."

"Then the door of communication should always be open," I said.

He nodded. "Both parties should continually be open and truthful."

"Indeed!"

"No coyness," he said.

"I think that what we need is an accountability partner," I suggested.

"How does that work?"

"It is about thinking long and hard," I said.

"It's about making a thoughtful decision," he offered.

"And having the right perspectives on issues."

Our temperaments were quite agreeable, and we seemed to care about each other. George visited my home, and my children were smitten with him.

My daughter whispered, "Will I be having two daddies?"

I was stupefied.

George invited us for lunch at his favorite restaurant. The children loved what he introduced us to, and they enjoyed his company. They listened to him and also contributed to the conversation. I watched in amazement as they behaved like they had known him all their lives. I concluded that he was good with them. I could tell he was a good father; he'd told me that he had a son from a first marriage. So we would become a blended family.

The boys were happy that I'd found someone who appreciated me. They said that they would be happy for him to be a part of the family.

But not so fast—George had to prepare. He had planned to start a business. For him, this appeared to be the best time. He called it "a time of new beginnings of great things." He had always loved the hospitality business and had a long-term plan, with men and materials in place, ready for takeoff.

On the family angle, we started a process of getting the needed accommodations and the long-term plan for our lives. I concentrated on planning what the children's days would be like.

My online store suffered. George offered to help me when needed. He documented our plans perfectly. I stood solidly behind him as he implemented his business action steps. It was tedious and cumbersome to undertake, but I was excited as I saw what was once a dream become reality. This was a world of possibilities opening for us. He was proposing a luxurious mid-range facility for an away-from-home experience for his guests, which would elicit repeat visits for the experience it offered. To achieve this, there were a series of meetings with contributors who were poised to work long and hard for the success of the idea.

George was also involved in reading and writing a lot of reports that were critical. I supported him as much as possible, even as we got key people to key positions to perform effectively. We worked hard, poring over details and asking questions from key personnel.

In all that we did, we made time for us and the children, and we always did something for ourselves that was critical as a couple and as a family. I was happy at how my life was unfolding.

"You are sunshine," George told me.

"You ignite the sunshine," I said.

Not long ago, George's son visited. The children had a splendid time together. Our family was formed. The children loved each other, and they loved us. George and I loved the children, and we loved each other.

Our plans coalesced in finding the ideal home for us all. I am a city girl; I have always lived in the city. He agreed to go along with my choice for a city life, and he spared no expense in making up the place for us all. We had a fantastic place to call home.

Then we told the priest to bless our union after our engagement party. It was a beautiful day when our families met. We started on a good note. George had succeeded in laying the framework for a thriving business, with the help of his associate.

With effort that exhibited his commitment to us, he made his presence felt at home. He was available to make an impact in our lives. He was considerate in making sure that there was balance between business and family time.

His arrangement has been truly blissful; we do have a splendid life!

Soon, the boys were ready for college. We provided them with books and materials needed to prepare for the qualifying exams. And we watched while encouraging them as they pored through the books. It was a tedious process, but they were tenacious and worked at understanding the difficult concepts. They never complained about doing their best, and their efforts were rewarded with good scores! They were admitted to the colleges of their choice.

Their move made me realize that I had come full circle. My children will be going away from home for a greater length of time than ever before. Just like my parents admonished me in my own time to be of good behavior on campus, I gave my boys my own words of wisdom, which was to eschew violence, and I prayed that it would be well with them.

We enjoined them to call home and keep us abreast of their lives. They had been good so far, so we believed that their transitioning to campus life would be better. They promised to be good and call often. We were happy and planned to have a family celebration during the holidays.

I looked at the happenings around me and realized that the children would be forming their own families soon. They had grown up to be good-natured people who appreciated all the goodness life had to offer. They are geared to working hard and are smart in their various callings, putting in the best effort and hoping for the best outcomes.

I can count my blessings. I have a love relationship in which we have built a stable home atmosphere—an example for the children to emulate. We plan to spend the remainder of our lives improving our business, a chore that will not be tedious; spending time with our grandchildren; traveling to learn and enjoy the beauty in the world; and impacting our community with information gathered. We plan to have a fun time as well—dining out and going out to dance occasionally for entertainment, reveling in music that lifts our souls and helps to show our gratefulness for having a great life.

Reading and gardening will also be part of our lives. We will also visit friends and family. To keep our interest alive, we will volunteer and continue to attend seminars to learn and contribute in our community. We will not limit ourselves but will continue to have an impactful life as counselors to those in need of our wisdom.

About the Author

Mary Agbotoh was born more than 50 years ago in Nigeria, West Africa. For the most part she lived her years in Lagos. That is where she got her elementary and high school education before proceeding to the western part of Nigeria for college. After college working as a reporter researcher, then as a supplements executive she relocated to the U.S. Ms. Agbotoh has always been interested in reading, and having read so much she knew she had to give back by writing about a topic of her interest.

Printed in the United States
by Baker & Taylor Publisher Services